America's Last Chance To Rock & Roll

An Essay On The State Of Our Nation

Written by

Alvin Brinkman, Jr.

ISBN-13: 978-1507822395
ISBN-10: 1507822391

DEDICATION

Dedicated to all the freedom fighters who came before me, and those who shall follow. Truth is a hard road and even more so in the search for and the defense of liberty.

CONTENTS

1
COLLAPSE OF THE AMERICAN DREAM

The collapse of the American Dream is eminent. The current world order could easily implode. If national law and order (as we know it) fail, it will unleash an overnight tsunami. Lush metropolises and once secure safe havens could become broken and deadly environments. The only minimally safe place will be locations where few care to go, and where life is hard but sustainable with minimal technology. What will emerge will be a new world power unlike any other, creating an entirely new set of hurdles and survival struggles. During such an apocalypse, one's exposure and proximity to the masses will increasingly be terminal for those living in populated urban environments. Desperation will transform the lives of everyone on this planet. Survival skills will be paramount but will not guarantee anything long term. Currently, there is a new centralized brutal world order, waiting for an opportunistic time to unleash its fury on the unaware populous that now contentedly sit on its loins and breeds. There remains one small window left to avoid this meltdown. America is one of few nations in the world that has the genetic code (DNA) capable of taking our republic back, bearing such consequences and righting the world we live in by example. However, time is short, the stakes continue to rise and the beast is growing more ruthless. What is waiting in the wings is not biblical. It is brought solely by the cumulative excess of human greed and power that have poisoned our water (so to speak) to such degree that it is no longer drinkable. The weight of the world is so great that it is (metaphorically) cracking. The "good and the evil" and the "beginning and the end" are both part of our current landscape and this discussion.

This essay is about America's last chance to "rock & roll" and on how we as a nation can be reborn. Anything short of a rigorous commitment will fail. This is a call to all of America's patriots of freedom.

2
MASS EQUALS DISINTEGRATION

The Second Law of Thermodynamics says spontaneous events increase disorder. Similarly, the weight and size of a mass rolling down a hill increases its rate of speed and destruction. I theorize that in civilization's the weight and size of populations determines the rate and speed of their cultural disintegration; referred to within as "Mass Equals Disintegration Theory" (m=d).

In all of the human history, civilizations began with a few and multiplied into masses. Problems arise when we apply the principles honed and developed in small group settings to large populations, resulting in a disintegration of the core values that made a system work in the first instance. In addition, m=d can be applied to every civilization known to man with similar results. Mass is a critical modifier of everything on our physical earth, why not on our civilizations?

Wondrous cultures existed within the magnificent ancient Mayan, Mesopotamian, Anasazi, and the medieval African empires of Mali and Songhai. History is abundant with examples of other extinct or demised empires all over the world such as the Greek, French, British, Italian and German world empires. Each of these civilizations began small and grew to world powers. Some civilizations have lived shorter lives than others, but none has by choice grown smaller, rather they have become larger than they ever imagined. With the relentless increase in the momentum of mass (populations), all systems become less efficient at everything and they eventually succumb to all manner of disintegration.

The m=d theory can be applied to America's population. In 1607 the Jamestown colony that had a relatively small beginning that evolved into the United States of America. In 1610, the estimated combined total populations of Plymouth and Virginia was 350 white settlers. By 1650, (only 40 years later) the combined total population of all the North American colonies was 50,368 (one of the highest birth rates in the world). In 1618, Virginia was composed of only eleven plantations. By 1700, the total population of the colonies was 250,888 and the total population of the world was 4,000,000 (4 million). In 2014, the total population of America (nationwide) had escalated to over 317 million (the fourth most populated nation in the world). In the space of 396 years, the population of our nation had increased from an estimated 350 people to over 317 million people (averaging an increase of 800,505 additional persons per year).

The m=d theory can also be applied to what is now called America's great experiment with its democratic republic.

On September 5, 1774, the *First Continental Congress* was composed of 56 delegates appointed by the legislatures of 12 of 13 colonies who met at Carpenter's Hall in Philadelphia, Pennsylvania. Their purpose was to discuss, among other issues, an economic boycott of British trade, rights, grievances, and to petition King George III for a British remedy to the colonies complaints.

In 1775, the *Second Continental Congress* met in Philadelphia after the *American Revolutionary War* (1775 to 1783) had already begun. Independence gained momentum, and Congress voted to approve the following:

1. In June of 1775, Congress approved and commissioned the *Continental Army* whose purpose was to defend the American colonies during the American Revolutionary War with the British Empire (Great Britain).

2. On July 4, 1776, Congress signed the *Declaration of Independence* declaring separation from Great Britain (drafted as a resolution by a committee of 5 congressional delegates and signed by 56 delegates).

3. On March 1, 1781, Congress drafted the *Articles of Confederation and Perpetual Union* (signed by 48 delegates). The Continental Congress was renamed the *Congress of the*

Confederation (Confederated Congress) which met from 1781 to 1788.

On June 21, 1788, the *Constitution of the United States* (5 pages long) was officially ratified by 9 of the 13 states that replaced the 1777 Articles of Confederation. Elected from the 13 states were 74 delegates to Congress (*Philadelphia Convention*) with 55 who attended and 39 who signed the Constitution creating a new federal government composed of the legislative, executive and judicial branches. The *United States Bill of Rights* was added as an amendment to the United States Constitution in 1791, when the Confederated Congress was renamed the *United States Congress.*

In 2015, the 114th *United States Congress* met in Washington, D.C. composed of 100 Senators and 435 members of the House of Representatives (totaling 535 members in Congress).

In summary, the population in America increased by 90 million percent from 1610 (350) to 2014, (317 million) and the number of colonial delegates and subsequently elected members of Congress has risen by 855 percent from 1774 (56 delegates) to 2015 (535 members in Congress). This massive population growth and government expansion make up only two components of the total picture of America's landscape. Further application of m=d to the monetary, industrial, environmental, legal, social, and educational aspects could be reasoned as to produce overwhelming obstacles and challenges no matter what form of government.

What once worked in 1774 is now buried in complexity and has for over 200 years demonstrated the strain and the disintegration of the culture of thought and process that first molded the framework of our nation. We the people have become weak sheep due to our growing ignorance of our U.S. Constitution multiplied by the decay of our cultural and moral fiber. Such a nature of being is not sustainable. The constitutional, political and social fissures in our society are some of the most critical issues our nation currently faces. And the application of m=d does not bode well for our survival, nor our status as a world superpower.

3
AMERICA'S ORIGINS & REBIRTH

The United States of America's origins began with sacrifices made by many of the original white colonists who came to this land for the purpose of enriching their fortunes. Half of those colonists arrived as indentured servitude laborers. Several years later the colonies established their independence and affirmed their inalienable rights. Now, more than 225 years later, our nation, which "we the people" formed, has succumbed to the dangers forecasted by our founders. Years of citizen apathy have fueled and multiplied the power of our state and federal governments. Regaining populous control of our governance is essential but it will not be easy, nor will it be quick. A concerted effort will require that we form a national unity of States led by patriots who are willing once again to accept the challenge of re-taking our hard fought rights, through legitimate means as authorized by our Constitution, and in keeping with the intent of our founding forefathers.

The process required to accomplish the goal of America's rebirth will be met with considerable opposition. Attempts to demonize the reform process will be punitive in order to protect the government's oppressive powers and its position of authority. Make no mistake regarding the immensely destructive and formidable forces that shall be unleashed upon reformers. Know that this struggle will divide our nation as if it were our countries second civil war. Casualties are inevitable, and the outcome is tenuous and risky. There will be those among us who will choose to be "rocks" set in stone supporting the hands that feed them. Alternatively, there will also be "rollers" who know that pushing the rocks over and out of the way is essential in order to regain control of our country for the purpose of preserving our constitutional freedoms. American's must now decide if they are capable or willing to engage in this cause. The outcome of their decision will make or break our nation. We have one last chance to "rock & roll."

Daniel Webster once said, "God grants liberty only to those who love it and are always ready to guard and defend it."

4
CONSTITUTIONAL REFORMS

In 1789, (14 years after the start of the American Revolutionary War of 1775) the seven articles of the Constitution of the United States of America were adopted. Authority for this document was cited in the preamble as "We, the people of the United States," and once ratified it became "the supreme law of the land." Federal law was declared, under specified authorized circumstances, as supreme over state laws. However, as originally intended federal supremacy only applied if Congress wrote federal laws allowed within the framework of the constitution. Congress (consisting of the United States Senate and the United States House of Representatives) has to date ratified 27 proposed amendments to the Constitution (including 10 amendments in the 1789 Bill of Rights) without rewriting the original constitution.

Scholars have argued for and against the doctrine that if Congress passes laws that states consider unconstitutional then such states have the right to nullify (invalidate) such federal law under the theory of nullification. Organizations such as the Tenth Amendment Center defend nullification citing its authority and purpose within the constitution.

James Madison wrote in the *Federalist Papers*,

"Should an unwarrantable measure of the federal government be unpopular in particular States, which would seldom fail to be the case, or even a warrantable measure be so, which may sometimes be the case, the means of opposition to it are powerful and at hand. The disquietude of the people; their repugnance (protests) and, perhaps refusal to cooperate with officers of the Union, the frowns of the executive magistracy of the State; the embarrassment created by legislative devices, which would often be added on such occasions, would oppose, in any State, very serious impediments; and were the sentiments of several adjoining States happen to be in Union, would present obstructions which the federal government would hardly be willing to encounter."

States have a constitutional right not to implement any federal law considered deemed by the states as "unwarrantable (unconstitutional) or unpopular." Using this option (currently known as the "New Nullification Movement") states can refuse to implement federal laws rendering such laws unenforceable. This movement is gaining speed and support in many states. Nullification appears to be the movement of choice for the reformation of our federal government and can be undertaken by individuals, communities, organizations, court juries and state legislatures.

Simply stated by James Madison this tool amounts to a "refusal to cooperate with officers of the Union." Furthermore, it has the power to stop laws, such as The Affordable Care Act, gun control, immigration reforms, or executive orders issued by the President, in their tracks.

However, the United States Supreme Court has struck down the Nullification Doctrine in favor of the Supremacy Clause, authorizing the Federal Court and Supreme Court to decide unconstitutional claims brought by states or persons against the federal government. The original 1789 constitution explicitly limited the powers of the federal government and granted the states "all remaining discretion to create laws they deemed necessary and prudent." A constitutional conflict arises when the application and definition of the articles in the constitution are arbitrarily decided by appointed justices of the United States Federal Courts or the United States Supreme Court without the consent of the populous. The federal government is not required by our constitution to govern by "consent of the states," but article five of the constitution grants states the power, by "application of two-thirds of the legislatures of the states" to hold constitutional amendment ratification conventions (last used in 1933 to ratify the 21st Amendment which repealed the 8th Amendment on the prohibition on alcohol) for the purpose of proposing amendments to the constitution that bypass Congress. In the application of this constitutional right of states, by way of the people, a majority of states can intervene in the affairs of the courts and Congress if Congress fails to adhere to the wishes of the people or exceeds congressional authority under the constitution. This process is cumbersome and costly but should not be dismissed or abandoned because it is central to popular and state votes and as such has a unique and definitive relationship to the people.

Never before has an American president or Congress so openly exceeded their constitutional authority. It is imperative that states convene constitutional amendment ratification conventions for the purpose of forming a foundation for the reform of our government. Our president, Congress, and all government bureaucracies need to be firmly reminded that they work for "We, the people of the United States" who paid the price to gain or independence and write and ratify our constitution. The people and the states must now step up and take our country back from the federal government and make us whole once again. The influence such federal reforms will have on the State Legislatures should not be understated. To do nothing now will continue to bring shame upon us all.

The well-known author, Mark R. Levin, has written several books on the United States Constitution and conservative principles. His well thought-out treatises outline the central issues at the heart of America's crisis and provide a pathway to begin creating solutions.

America's Last Chance to Rock & Roll: An Essay on the State of Our Nation offers several essential constitutional reforms required for the rebirth of America.

1.   A four-year election term with a two successive life-term limit shall be set for Congress and the House of Representatives who shall be elected simultaneously. The Senators shall be appointed by, and answer to the State Legislatures as originally intended in the Constitution, and the House of Representatives shall be elected by and answer to the people. A national election format shall be established by Congress where all national candidates would have open access to debate, in accessible

public forums, at no cost to the candidates. Each national candidate must quarterly declare all funds raised and the named sources of same in a national registry to include all corporate, non-corporate and personal or private donations or other sources of campaign revenues received, without exception.

2. Ten-year term limits shall be installed for federal and supreme court justices who shall be appointed by Congress and whose opinions shall be subject to congressional review or by a super majority of state legislatures, who shall have the authority to annul or reverse any federal or supreme court decisions by a two-thirds majority vote.

3. Congress shall adopt a fiscal federal budget not to exceed receipts from its fiscal gross national product. All current federal income tax and wage deductions shall be repealed. Congress shall enact a bilateral ten-percent national flat tax on for-profit and non-profit corporations, religious entities, independent social agencies and all individuals based on their gross income receipts. Congress shall enact a 10% consumption and use tax on all goods and services purchased by the above entities, and individuals. All foreign and domestic corporations, entities, and individuals shall pay a ten-percent federal tax on the sale of any and all real-estate holdings on transfer of such deeds. No federal tax increases shall be levied except by a majority of Congress. A national referendum shall be held to determine if the people approve temporary, specific cuts in national services and agencies, which savings must be used only for the purpose of reducing the accumulated national debt. If approved, such law shall permanently expire on a given date and the federal government held publicly accountable for such laws fulfillment.

4. State and federal governments (or its agents) shall not seize private property by "eminent domain" or the "taking clause," or restrict the value by "reclassification" or assume possession of any person's property (real estate or land) without paying just compensation at full market value prior to any taking for public use.

5. Double taxation regarding estate inheritances shall be abolished and cannot be passed on to future generations.

6. The Federal Reserve Bank of America shall return to the "gold standard," and shall present its fiscal and monetary

policies to Congress for approval by majority vote. The Federal Reserve Bank of America and all other banks conducting financial transactions of any kind in America shall hold their assets in America in gold and shall not conduct any electronic transactions that are not secured and verified by such gold reserves.

7. Congress shall reduce the entire existing federal civil workforce by fifty-percent. All current federal paid holidays shall be terminated, federal unions abolished and all federal salaries shall be based on reasonable comparative salaries in the private sector as set by Congress.

8. The United States Federal Department of Education shall be abolished, and the functions of education returned to the States. Lifetime tenure shall be abolished, and all educators evaluated based on performance. Multi-cultural education and bilingual education shall be abolished, and English restored as our single national language.

9. Current immigration policies shall be abolished and reformed by Congress to include removing any existing presidential decrees, chain migration birth laws for non-citizens, rights to alien drivers licenses, rights to alien social security benefits and medical treatments, rights to alien social programs, and there shall be no amnesty for current illegal aliens. Immigration must be restricted to individuals with the ability to contribute to this society. All current illegal aliens must report to immigration, or they shall be arrested, forfeit all rights and property, and be incarcerated until their speedy deportation. All borders shall be secured and locked down until Congress approves their re-opening. The staff of all foreign embassies, members of all foreign governments and associations who are not citizens of America must be asked to leave or be deported until such time as Congress approves their presence; all such foreign ambassadors or agents shall be held accountable to the laws of the United States of America, without exception. Foreign flags shall not be flown in government or public institutions. All illegal aliens who have been arrested for criminal offenses shall be removed from state and federal prisons, stripped of any and all rights, identified by DNA and retina scans, transported to a secure holding facility and permanently deported to their country of origin in an expedited manner.

10. Any and all national health care laws such as the Affordable Care Act of 2010 must be repealed because they are unconstitutional and illegal. All health care decisions shall be returned to the people and the private sector. Medicare, Medicaid, Supplemental Income, Social Security, Disability and all other welfare forms of entitlement programs must be re-examined by Congress and altered in significant ways so as to make them sustainable or to abolish said entitlements. Congress shall be charged with the review of all entitlements, shall report to the people on why any entitlements have failed to be sustainable or reasonable and shall propose alternative programs as needed.

11. Congress and the federal government shall refrain from establishing or enforcing any laws that constrain or restrict public speech, radio and television, or the internet.

12. Congress shall abolish the Veterans Administration, Department of Veteran Affairs, and the Secretary of Veteran Affairs office. Congress shall reconstruct and streamline a new United States Veteran Administrative Agency to manage a National Veteran Health Insurance Program policy whereby each and every veteran is provided with a national insurance policy card that shall be recognized in any and all health care systems and facilities in America and those participating abroad. The Veteran Administration shall be stripped of all health care functions, and battlefield medical attention shall be implemented by the armed forces until such time as a veteran is transferred or discharged from military service. Congress shall abolish all current laws regarding the budget of the Veterans Administration and shall fund the new United States Veteran Administrative Agency through the federal budget process, not by appropriations based on the whims of Congress or the president. Eligibility for veteran disability claims shall be adjudicated by a contract agency authorized by Congress with the mandate to expedite and settle all claims within 60 days and any appeals to such claims shall be adjudicated or settled in civilian courts within one year.

The processes of constitutional amendment ratification conventions and annulment through nullification cannot be ignored. Once organized and executed, the implications of such process will make history and will revitalize the democratic process.

Robert Yates said,

"But remember, when the people once part with power, they can seldom or never resume it but by force. Many instances can be produced in which the people have voluntarily increased the powers of their rulers, but few, if any, in which rulers have willingly abridged their authority. This is a sufficient reason to induce you to be careful, in the first instance, how you deposit the powers of government."

John Adams once said,

"Power always thinks it has a great soul and vast views beyond the comprehension of the weak."

James Baldwin remarked,

"But the relationship between morality and power is a very subtle one. Because ultimately power without morality is no longer power."

In the *Federalist Essay* by Alexander Hamilton, John Jay, and James Madison said,

"If angels were to govern men, neither external nor internal controls on government would be necessary. In framing a government which is to be administered by men over men, the great difficulty lies in this: you must first enable the government to control the governed; and in the next place oblige it to control itself."

At the conclusion of the Philadelphia Constitutional Convention of 1789, Benjamin Franklin was asked,

"What have you given us? It is a Republic, now let's see if you can keep it."

"Only a virtuous people are capable of freedom. As nations become corrupt and vicious, they have more need of masters."

5
EXHAUSTION BY DESIGN PRINCIPLE

The "Exhaustion by Design Principle" (EDP) is defined within as governmental procedural force applied to an appellant who seeks to affirm his or her rights under the United States Constitution.

EDP is an operational phrase for a method of coercion used by highly sophisticated systems of governance with one primary goal: control and containment of opposition to a policy. It is a widely used and a carefully executed method of social engineering that encourages dissenters and opponents of policy to engage in a discourse with governmental bodies that formally hear and review complaints by appellants seeking remedy for their concerns. Often, such hearings are referred to as an expression of one's rights. In theory, this model is used by devious practitioners and is allusively deceiving. One of the principle requirements set forth to exercise one's rights is the full disclosure of your identity (including one's financial status). Few appellants ever consider the effect such disclosure will have on their future in the civil culture within which they live. Rights do not guarantee results, which is the most misunderstood myth of our current republic's evolution. Many social and behavioral studies have shown that humans will reach a state of exhaustion, become weak, and vulnerable to relentless stress. No swords need be drawn to accomplish this effect if the system of governance establishes a lawful maze of seemingly harmless hurdles for appellants to jump through as they exercise their rights. Once an appellant is exhausted, the oppositional threat of a person is minimized, if not smothered. Even after an appellant's defeat, the system offers yet further venues, such as right to appeal. EDP destroys an appellants' inertia and eventually renders them harmless to the system; it is one of the most benign yet powerful social engineering tools ever exercised in human history. The use of the EDP is so pervasive in most highly civilized cultures that it has become the norm; without opposition or discussion, it is used for suppressing anything and everything!

During the processing of one's rights, the government redirects an appellant's vital human energy and resources to an endless string of bureaucratic prerequisites arbitrarily set to limit the expression of these rights. The simple but direct language used in our 1789 Bills of Rights has over time, become convoluted by numerous governmental interpretations and lengthy procedural entanglements so that these rights have become severely diminished in the process. Remedy is no longer possible without a team of lawyers at one's disposal. Extensive legal and unwarranted encumbrances ultimately render the appellant physically drained and financially ruined. This appellant then leaves the struggle in a state of bewilderment and dismay. Given this circumstance, an appellant is highly unlikely ever to approach such a task again.

EDP is so effective at suppression that its use has migrated by chapter and verse into every corner of governance. Such a system is not free, not just, and certainly not equal. Such a practice is appalling and disgusting especially as it purports to be the proper and orderly execution of one's rights under the constitution. Nowhere in the framework of the Bill of Rights is there the language to support this aberration yet state and federal statutes have affirmed this policy. What manner of man would devise such hurdles to fundamental rights but the bureaucrats and politicians who seek only to protect the structures they have thus accumulated and to disparage those who seek just remedy?

There appears but one way to correct this festering wound, and that is simply to cut off the legs of our legal system of governance. Not by revolts or embarking upon endless judicial wrangling fraught with EDP barriers, but by mandating through Congress that all state and federal courts must hear, adjudicate, and settle all claims brought before it within a prescribed minimalistic and reasonable time. If claims are not properly adjudicated or settled within that time, then the appellant shall be granted its claim. In addition, reasonable claims brought against the state or federal government by a common citizen or group of citizens shall carry no fees to initiate a claim but be it at a state or federal expense. Such laws, if enacted by Congress, would have immediate and sweeping effects that would motivate state and federal governments to remove any EDP impedances they have set, so as to avoid their liability or punitive damages. In short order, the unwarranted and complicated world of state and federal law, as they apply to constitutional rights, would come to an end, and the rights of citizens would be restored. Prudence would prevail within statutory law, and the burden of proof would be equalized. At first, this change in policy would create a drain on government resources, but eventually, the ebb and flow of this initial busy traffic would wane, sanity would be restored to governance and rights would be equally accessible to all. There is no anarchy alarm to be heard in this initiative but for the sound of trumpets declaring a renewed democratic republic with only blue sky above.

Samuel Adams stated,

"The sum of all is, if we would most truly enjoy the gift of Heaven, let us become a virtuous people; then shall we both deserve and enjoy it. While, on the other hand, if we are universally vicious and debauched in our manners, though the form of our Constitution carries the face of the most exalted freedom, we shall in reality be the abject slaves."

6
THE IDEAL IDEA CONCEPT

From the ancient genetic camaraderie of early philosophers begat the first written forms of conscious thought regarding the process of civil culture and intellectual property. Doctrines soon proliferated from those who followed, and in due course, abundant treatises arrived for their many followers. Then, as now, there is no shortage of scholars who will profess to have discovered secrets of the divine and paths that guarantee everything, including eternity. It seems curious that so many ideas portend perfect solutions to human misery, but we remain miserable in spite of their edicts. The "Ideal Idea" concept explores the human mind, as it searches for what is right and just and offers a place where we can go to and be protected from ourselves.

Ideas are what man fears most because each of us knows that we are capable of great harm, to anything, yet we cannot hide from having thoughts. Great thinkers have no such human frailties, fears or boundaries because they are prone to be self-indulgent tyrants, dictators and princes of the realm of wisdom. The gift of intellectual speech is often discovered at a young age, and the persuasion it offers perpetuates its prevalence. The less gifted have no such immunity or power and must find a way to tame their thoughts to a manageable state that offers them refuge, which then prompts them to begin the search for their individual ideal idea that each will use to navigate through their journey.

Conformity is the most commonly adopted ideal idea because it comes in many forms and like a fast food, it is easily consumable and comes in many disguises, shrouded in religion, politics, science, philosophy, money, war, racism. By coincidence, each food type is said to be far superior to all others. No matter which we choose, each requires a devotion that creates a bond between the idea and the self that is seldom broken, except under great pain and suffering. This bond is the price paid to hide behind one's shadow.

Conformers believe that we can take the chaos out of mankind (as if such a thing was possible) only if there is order, and that such order is usually a privilege only afforded by government. This notion is a convenient truism for most: if one only follows instructions, most individual intellectual liability and accountability will be grouped with the many, who then will bear responsibility for all resulting actions.

However, man is designed and wired to explore, not to conform, and soon the group splinters first by a few, and then by many in directions that tempt their fate, and ultimately form their destiny. The chains of conformity break under the weight of the illusion of an idea whose function is dependent on the many. When illusion is unveiled disillusion follows, and we are left once again with the real nature of man. Given the opportunity, we each could indeed be closeted beasts, murderers, tyrants, frauds of faith and merchants of misery. And, when we see once again what our true nature is, we go back in search of the ideal idea. Man has in his heart the notion that his store might be empty when winter comes, thus leading to panic and diminishing faith in his self-reliance. Fear grows with hunger that is both evident and perceived. It takes surviving a winter to know how to manage its threat. Additionally, the courage and understanding required to assume such a task is not easy when we learn that the ordeal could be lethal.

There comes a time when each of us should just lay at the side of the road. A time when the direction of the wind, and the graceful movements of the clouds becomes one's chosen angle of passage.

Such exceptional moments will have no tending priests nor burning crosses. One is alone, in quiet, with only the spirit of discovery.

In this graceful peace, the sole removes itself from the fusion of things to the cellular level of being and you are warm inside.

Dissuasion from traditional formats of conformity may mean a change in direction and criticism by small people looking to pierce your armor.

But have no fear, you are now in the vaulted depths of creation. What better place on Earth is there to be?

7
LAW & ORDER

The Police State will, in time, be upon us and shall grow exponentially to control the reckless desperadoes who will live among preying on us. Most police come from a working class citizen base and know what its like to live with the people. As in any field, there are those in law enforcement who are predators and loose cannons. A review of the individual performance of the majority of police officers will reveal that compassion and constraint are also in the mix. It is, for this reason, unwarranted to degrade the authority of those we authorize to take up arms to protect our lives at the risk of their own. Somewhere we need to find peace with the law unless we are bent on breaking it.

Our greatest looming threat is how our police culture manages the anticipated transformation from civil law enforcement to Marshal Law. If prudence prevails, excessive force will be the exception. However, any combat veteran will tell you that conditioning denies reason. If civil law is degraded to any degree, there will be a new police culture of rule that will implode and explode, from within and outside our safe zones. This change in enforcement attitudes is already occurring in many European and Third World countries and will soon visit our shores with a vengeance. Unrest will manifest in many ways, and most Americans will not be ready. When chaos occurs liberals will ask for protection from armed citizens and the instinct to survive will trump all logic. Out of this misery, there will come a shining star. The divisive tendencies of worthless politics will blend into a sense of community and out of this bittersweet moment we will find each other again. It should be clear to those whose heads are not buried in the sand that preparation is no longer an option but a necessity, and even the best prepared may not survive.

It is thus recommended that all American's arm themselves, as they did prior to independence, under the Second Amendment to assure they can defend their liberty. Such action is paramount.

8
FOREIGN POLICY

The world is forever changing and adapting. America's foreign policy theater is far too complicated, mismanaged, unsustainable and extremely costly. Congress must take immediate action to cut funds for reckless foreign policy agendas. Presidential powers need to be reined in and justified by a measurable accounting of the cost-benefit relationship with every foreign country that feeds from the American plate. All foreign aid programs should be halted indefinitely until each application is reviewed and approved by Congress without exception. All United States embassies and government offices in foreign countries should be closed indefinitely and secured until Congress reviews and approves their purpose and budget.

No United States president shall have the authority to authorize any military agency to engage any enemy in an act of war without prior approval from Congress, without exception. Congress must be fully prepared immediately to review any pending conflict or presidential request and to respond to such event with the utmost expediency. The president must be assured that access to Congress will be forthcoming at all times and that any presidential request must be taken up and reviewed without party prejudice. Our military defense organizations must be fully funded to stand ready and able with the most advanced military equipment on earth. We must never allow another Pearl Harbor or 9-11. We must also refrain from engagements that could be managed by defensive intelligence and technology. Boots on the ground should be a last resort and only if approved by Congress. America's current role as a superpower that traverses the world to engage all manner of perceived threats should be abolished. Such global responsibility is no longer wise, prudent or sustainable. In addition, a reasonable mandatory draft system should be implemented to divide the duty of serving this nation among all citizens of America, both rich and poor. Why are veterans rare in Congress these days?

9
THE FEDERAL GOVERNMENT

The Federal Reserve Bank of America has morphed into a renegade self-contained bombshell that is accountable to no one. All federal agencies must be reorganized, vetted, funded and regulated by Congress. No federal agency shall be unaccountable to the people. The people and Congress have neglected to responsibly oversee the federal government and must reclaim their jurisdiction. Transparency and sense of mission have been skewed with layers of complexity seldom understood by anyone. Fear of government and its powers diminish both purpose and accountability. No one agency should have impunity or a monopoly on the intelligence required to execute its functions. One needs only to look at the recent bailouts of America's banks and automotive industries to realize that no one is guarding the people's money.

Federal policies on printing money to no end and making unsecured electronic funds available to elite banking sectors behind closed doors must cease. The American dollar must return to the gold standard. Banks must end the practice of electronic speculative loans without gold assets to cover defaults. No taxpayer funds should be used to prevent bank failures. Let the chips fall where they may, and let's get on with proper and responsible banking on a community level that invests where such banks do business. Offshore accounts for all banks operating in America must be prohibited. Consumers must take charge of where they put their money. All banks are not created equal, and some are simply a pariah.

Samuel Adams once said,

"If ye love wealth better than liberty, the tranquility of servitude than the animated contest of freedom, go from us in peace. We ask not your counsels or arms. Crouch down and lick the hands which feed you. May your chains sit lightly upon you, and may posterity forget that you were our countrymen!"

10
THE ECONOMY

The two most urgent aspects of our economy are tax reform and employment. Our federal tax code is corrupted, unsustainable, and unjust. The solution is a maximum uniform ten percent flat tax that everyone (individual, corporate or non-profit) must pay on all gross income with no deductions and no loopholes. The Internal Revenue Service should be downsized by seventy-five percent of its forces, with the remainder of its agents designated to field enforcement. All corporations (including non-profits and religious holdings) should pay equal taxes based on their real-estate asset values and gross income from any and all sources. America's tax house needs to be re-ordered.

In addition, Congress should immediately proceed to readjust its budget so that it is limited to projected revenues minus substantial investments towards the reduction of the current unsustainable deficit. America, like other nations, should look at its debt to determine if our default on debt is warranted. All programs receiving federal funding must be re-certified, bonded, altered as needed and monitored to assess compliance. No state or federal laws should be enacted without adequate and defined public review and discussion. Bills in Congress and State Legislatures must be purpose-specific and limited to 5,000 words.

In addition, Congress must retrain our workforce making them more suitable for new technology industries. Trade schools need to be reintroduced at the high school and community level. We as a nation need to examine other industrial and technology-driven global states and replicate their successes. Our educational system has failed to develop a culture of learning that meets the demands of our economy. Education particularly at the college level needs total reform and reorganization. We can no longer call higher education learning. Universities are not serving our nation but rather themselves. Nothing short of major renovations to the basics of our economy and educational structures will be of any use.

11
SOCIAL PROGRAMS

Medicare and Social Security are legacy programs that made promises to millions of Americans and such promises must be kept. If such programs can no longer be sustainable due to rising costs, then Congress should end the programs for new recipients and buy out those who wish to terminate the program. However, if the budget and the deficit are brought under control and the economy has the strength required then Congress must revise Medicare, Medicaid and Social Security to meet strict criteria, such as income limits, asset limits, and estate and capital asset transfers to reduce recipients to the most needy (not the general public). Medicare and Medicaid payroll tax deductions shall be abolished as they are the taking of money by the federal government under the disguise of insurance. All such federal programs must seek reauthorization from Congress.

Social welfare programs have been abused for decades in America and have drained civil resources and institutionalized welfare into a means of living. Disability programs have spiraled out of control as liberal markers have replaced common sense. America needs to look carefully at all social welfare programs to make all agencies lean and accountable. A national debate needs to occur regarding the American work ethic and individual responsibility for contributing to one's sustenance and fundamental survival. Racial divides have plagued our nation too long. Racism should no longer be recognized as an institution. Rather, it needs to be put to sleep, for the betterment of our nation. Bite the bullet, and move on.

Feeding America's hungry (especially our young children and elderly) should be our primary mission. Surely this country can afford to feed its needy citizens if they cannot feed themselves. Basic food sustenance is a fundamental human obligation we must meet (at all cost). Housing, on the other hand, is problematic, and many past interventions have failed. Thus, we have our American ghetto. Employment is the preferred option to social unrest and misery. We need to put American's to work. What a novel solution?

12
POLITICAL REFORMS

As a prerequisite to the principles of re-birthing America, Congress must repeal the 17th Amendment and reinstate Article 1, Section 3. The United States Senate should not be elected by the people, but by state legislatures (independent of the populous) to best represent the interests of each state in the United States Senate. Congress must also establish a national system of election reforms to include a National Election Fund providing common citizens with an incentive to participate as candidates in national electoral processes. All federal candidate donations must be declared so as to render a fair and equal platform for all contenders. The United States Senate and House of Representatives must be appointed and elected simultaneously (not separately by segregated term election mandates), so as to prevent the political division of Congress and for the purpose of minimizing election costs. Senator and representative terms shall not exceed four years or two consecutive life terms.

The founding fathers and the people intended that elected office be temporary in nature and not permanent. Rotation in elected positions is inconvenient but critical in responding to the nature of change in government and social reform. For too long politicians have roosted in their cages as monarchs of their jurisdictions. It is time to test the men and women we have nurtured to see if they have been groomed well enough to preserve the republic on which we stand. If this is not the case, the reason for any such failure must be righted until being a patriot is once again established. Politics is a living thing that requires fresh ideas in response to new needs. The greed and power now bestowed on a few elitist politicians must end. Power begets power, and special interest lobbyists own far too many political figures who in the course of service have lost their ambition to lead by example according to the demands of the people. Congress is not a permanent place to put one's hat. It is more like public service on a temporary platform that fulfills patriotic and community service ambitions. This model is lost in the existing excesses of the current power structure built by only a few individuals that have betrayed the American people in pursuit of personal gain. Every patriotic citizen in America knows this to be fact but has to date not moved to correct it. The result is a runaway federal government that mocks and demonizes anyone who calls their bluff and challenges their conduct. Such arrogance is proof of the rampant expansion of such legislative disregard. Congress has gone mad and lost the faith of American's at large. We the people need to close this door and expunge such tyrants from the bowels of our republic.

Voting citizens must ask hard questions on federal reforms and hold political wannabes accountable for their actions. "Voting the bums out" replaces one bum with another. New electoral candidates are currently no guarantee of change. Sound bites and polished political slogans must be identified and averted. Debates need to be set on fire. The engagement of political diversity and the end to the two-party-rule needs to be forthcoming. Not because it is controversial, but because it has no intrinsic value beyond that of discriminatory behavior displayed by eccentrics who have no idea of what community means and whose lives revolve around self-interest. To those latter individuals, I compel you to know that you are shameful and degrading.

Daniel Webster stated,

"It is hardly too strong to say that the Constitution was made to guard the people against the dangers of good intentions....There are men, in all ages....who mean to govern well; but they mean to govern. They promise to be kind masters; but they mean to be masters....They think there need be but little restraint upon themselves....The love of power may sink too deep in their own hearts..."

Thomas Jefferson said,

"The good sense of the people will always be found to be the best army. They may be led astray for a moment, but will soon correct themselves."

13
MORAL ACCOUNTABILITY

Our temple of liberty begs for a new and fresh expression. America must reflect on what we have lost in our search for wealth and recognize our dehumanization by way of technology. We have surrendered the character that once defined us. No longer can we ascribe to edicts that have long since poisoned our retrospection, sedated our instincts and set us into a night of sleep from which we have yet to awaken. Tools not used rust and become extinct as has our individual self-respect. We by greed and moral decay have lost sight of the importance of diversity in thought. In addition, we have trashed and trampled critical social principles such as a person's word. Honesty is now seen as a weakness, and our higher social order stands defiled. Weak moral restraint is a plague on our self-identity and carries with it sickness that is contagious; this rendering it by definition an urgent issue requiring aggressive actions.

Religion has been contentious throughout America's history, and rightly so. What subject, save politics, can turn neighbors and brothers against each other in a battle of passion so severe that it has no remedy? Tolerance must remain apportioned to even those designated as heretics. The process of spiritual commitment is emotional, hypnotic and truistic. In practice, one's faith can also supersede logic; of this, it is often guilty. Nothing is immune from human intervention. Introspection is not heretical but cleansing. Be who you are, not what you are pressured to become. Evil has many definitions but is always discernible. Good is the intent to do right that does not profit at the expense of another's misery. These opposing legions have been at combat for eternity in all forms of humanity and governance. Such is our condition.

John Adams said,

"Our constitution was made only for a moral and religious people. It is wholly inadequate to the government of any other."

14
SUMMARY

All known empires and mighty civilizations throughout eternity have eventually expired, dried up or were conquered and extinguished. America will be no exception to this rule. Our nation's decline is questionable. There is still an opportunity to do the hard work needed to preserve our destiny and to get our house in order.

The principles contained in this essay do not seek to dismantle or degrade our constitution or our republic. Rather, they reinforce our founding principles and the genius of our constitution. A careful read of the *Federalist Papers* and our *constitution* will show that solutions submitted within this essay are faithful to the founder's intent and the people's mandate, both then, and now.

Right and wrong, good and evil, are not as complicated as philosophers and theologians would have us believe. Most of us are born with a sufficient matrix (DNA) to decide what line we cross or defend. Everyone (regardless of our genes) ultimately determines this equation at some point in time. And no one can escape its mortal grip or social and civil responsibility. We are all potential scoundrels, some of us live with demons, and others talk to God; yet, as a species, we are all in the universal natural process of dying (our last effort). What matters is to what degree and nothing else.

Honestly, I must admit my heart holds little faith that America has the wisdom and mainly the fortitude to meet the challenges discussed within. The premise of freedom and liberty has been so homogenized that it has lost its value. I hope I am mistaken, and that our nation lives long and well into the future. But if it does not, remember this discussion.

Listen, if you can, to the song of loon's as they settle into the night. The joy in their expression is the definition of freedom. Humans on this planet need to reassemble their priorities and move to reaffirm the center of our origins. We have not strayed by design

26

from truth; we have stayed by fictional deceit from which we appear defenseless.

Good is not a difficult choice, but rather a personal ambition. Likewise, evil is the same. We are, by default, left with a prevalence of the latter, and there seems to be no remedy. The plenty of evil is evidence that good is not as profitable, yet many hold the moral high-ground without question. Practitioners of evil and deceit are in endless supply and always will be part of the human condition. It is the moral duty of the good to remain vigilant within this circumstance.

We are once again writing a journal of what we were, are now, and might become. In time, this will be referred to as history. Blame will be rampant and accountability minuscule. In the end, as always, good shall prevail because good is the universal sustenance of man. However, it will also come at a high price and will be wrought with sacrifice.

Why in America's diverse history, have constitutional values been so obscured in the course of our republic's progression? What other truths have we lost? Such inquisition should be followed by the proposition that we have for so long been led, that we cannot lead, nor do we possess sufficient patriots willing to take on the challenge of our nation's rebirth. As a people, we have for the most part resigned to be followers, and for that purpose we are well endowed.

There is no right destiny for man, only the one that prevails; this is what separates us from other species. This also shows that our profound inadequacies can often lead to our demise. The product of man should not be measured by endurance, but by the quality of the reign of its realm.

"Popular law" is not "populous law." That which is popular is brought by media. Populous is by vote of the majority. These are seldom the same and are often misunderstood. What is presented by most media is not sincere, but rather indigenous to what power they are paid by and what they would have you believe. Be confident you know upon which you rely. The world, as we know it, and our nations longevity is at stake.

There is no known eternal order of man that can claim any permanent rein on humanity beyond its time on earth. And time has no boundaries. The notion, that one is more right than another is of insignificance in the evolution of man. What occurs in the nature of what we are is not what we became but what we perceive that we are or will become. No nation (including America) has a monopoly on democracy, and neither have we done all things correctly.

Many countries continue to experiment with evolving democratic and dictatorial possibilities. The outcome of each depends on the intent of the mission. Each mission should be judged by its ambitions. Such is the history of man. America does not currently have a national dialog regarding what constitutes new threats against our democratic republic; rather, we are entrenched in old ideas and allegiances that blur our vision. The definition of citizenry has been so diluted that it is no longer part of our vocabulary. As a result of our apathy, we've grown weak and pale compared to who we were when we became a nation.

Our flag has been soiled by liberalism, and the ability to assimilate is in question by foreign immigrants. To this folly, we impede our democratic progress, demolish our republic's mission and leave us broken and vulnerable to the desires of a few who disregard the many noble, yet lethargic, real citizens of our nation. It is time "we the people" stand up for our principles, shake off neutrality, and replace it with stern dispositions that display actions which deliver a message that we (America) are tired of standing on the shore watching our mother-ship sink. In order to move our nation into a positive position, all the citizens of America (young, old, rich, poor) need to engage the wheels to move our republic in a forward direction and without apology. I for one have had enough of being nice and neutral.

Our Republic cannot, and should not, be directed otherwise than to be stern, demanding of each other and of the nation that we should work hard to make amends and solidify our differences for the benefit of us all. There is no other way for our country to proceed. To do otherwise will lead to anarchy by the omission of the will of strength and fortitude. Such is not who we are, as I am lead to believe.

Thomas Jefferson noted,

"We in America do not have government by the majority, we have government by the majority who participate.... All tyranny needs to gain a foothold is for people of good conscience to remain silent."

James Madison remarked,

"A well-instructed people alone can be permanently a free people."

This essay could go on infinitely. The subject matter contained within has been enumerated by countless much more qualified authors than I. But take note, that I, a member of a great accumulative puzzle, consider my vote paramount, and I shall not leave these matters to questionable others, which is so commonly done by so many who couch themselves in sheepish self-interests.

We in America are a people once known for our revolutions and evolutions. We (as a cumulative of many cultures) ultimately owe our allegiance to the deposits of which we claim as our national heritage (wealth). Thus, in theory, no-one has any wealth but for the hard work of the people of the original Republic as a whole, certainly not illegal immigrants who lack the desire to assimilate into us. Even alien cultures would claim the same as their principles while living in their homelands. So why should it be different here in America?

I take great interest in how genuinely concerned American's take positions on issues that are far apart from other interpretations and stands on how and what we need to do for the purpose of making positive change. In many ways, we as a nation are divided in this endeavor. Each of us seemingly cares, with varying degrees of compassion, about our country yet we walk different paths and see different solutions. It is the same dilemma that led our country into it's American Civil War (1861 to 1865) that took the lives of 650,000 American soldiers. From what source did we inherit this divisional curse? I believe in diversity of thought and consideration of others views, and I find discussions to be learning events. But I also have witnessed fewer people who want to share their opinions with others or discuss issues of disagreement. Most people take the position that they must defend, not learn.

I see some dark reasons why we as a culture live with and perpetuate evil. I fear evil is hard-wired in the genes of mankind and is not simply a misguided state of mind.

As a closing remark I ask you to remember the words of Joni Mitchell, "Don't it always seem to go, you never know what you've got till it's gone."

15
ABOUT THE AUTHOR

It took me 65 years to write this essay, which I began constructing the day I was conceived. Like most newborns, my neurons were at first over-amped as I started burning images and events into my memory. Fast forward all these years later to when I finally decided that I had indeed gathered many photographs and memorable events of my life into a cerebral album that is now running out of space. I decided to share my experiences with the world before I depart, and my album is erased.

Because of the sensitive and direct nature of what I present here, I think it appropriate that readers know an outline of my biography. I was born in Wisconsin during a cold winter in 1949 and spent most of my childhood living with my family in a low-income neighborhood. My parents were white, uneducated, and they struggled to meet the debts incurred while raising their three children. Although I did not live in severe poverty, my social upbringing certainly was not middle class or above. Education was my youthful occupation, which I succeeded in with mediocre results. Later, I obtained a university degree. I am not a philosopher or scholar. I am honored to be a "Conservative Commoner."

During my upbringing, our parents were careful not to influence us with prejudices or shield us from social issues. My extended ancestors were immigrant naturalized citizens, mostly of the Christian faith. I was taught honesty, frequently disciplined and knew right from wrong. I was a happy child and never neglected or abused.

In 1967, I enlisted in the United States Army at the naive age of 18 and served in combat in Vietnam from 1968 to 1969. Afterward, life for me was never the same. Then, as now, I questioned everything and followed no one. Politics, religions, and sciences are all subjects that warrant introspection. It is with this spirit that I present this essay as an accumulation of my life's learning. I am proud of who I am, and I feel lucky to be an American.

When I was young, I fought hard for America's freedoms (but I was figuratively blind then, and less blind now). I sense a genuine resurgence of national patriotism in our country, but not to the level it needs to be in order to sustain our liberty. Every citizen needs to contribute to our collective identity to the extent that such effort is useful, not just to pretend on occasion, when convenient. May the gods of the universe bless all of our soldiers, our police, and their families, for all time. Without them, we would be chained amongst those who would conquer us. And conquer they would. Freedom is not a game. Hearken to your heart of hearts, if you have one. It should be telling you to sound an alarm. Be wise and listen to such message, or be consumed by the foe that is waiting in your doorway.

PATRIOTS

LEAVE YOUR MARK

ANY MARK

TAKE BACK OUR NATION!